TexasNationalGangstersInc

Jamie David Jesuitas

21ˢᵗ CENTURY REVOLUTION

a true story authored, narrated & screen played
by: San JDJesuitas

Table of contents:

SYNOPSIS: The TexasNationalGagstersInc decisive objective is to remove the drug violence from their own sovereign Texas borders, and send the blood-shed back to Columbia and Peru where it originates. The ultimate motives will be to expose the underworld, and clench the illicit narcotics-trafficking in their own back yards. Gangster Vice-chairman San Glenn agreed that all these goals will be achieved easily enough, once these tactics are published, since the best way to exploit such paranormal-feats is to hire the adversaries' mercenaries, to defect and start from within.

So by publishing all resolutions in a reverse propaganda styled format, it will be easy enough to recruit criminals as auxiliary forces under command. Obviously, it will become increasingly realistic, once on the inside, to gain access without violence, thru cooperative efforts, to all the undocumented weapons, illicit drugs, and laundered money within the Texas National Boundaries.

Introduction: There is fortunately an alternative form of *"Free-enterprise Self-governing"* that is now emerging under the authority of Texas National Independence, and which will further restore confidence in Texas national sovereignty and security. As the US economy further disintegrates, this Texas super-power arising, in corollary, has apparently not been the cause of America's demise, but will in turn become the recourse. This better choice will increasingly attract overall and sundry; and so now everyone can play their part guiltless, with superfluity of guile and utmost confident acuity.

Most Americans actually still believe the stratagem of the CIA is to safeguard national security in the USA. This may have been true at one time. But reprehensibly, for quite some time now, a global dogma of mega-wealthy international exponents, who head-up the federal-reserve, and pull all the strings, behind the scenes, on the US government, are further intent on controlling the world economy at great national loss. This influential group of international tycoon thugs have continually bought & sold our USA elected lawmakers, to their own agenda, and now at great cost to America's national freedom and national security.

All the financial foreign-aid packages, the USA gives away to governments of other countries, all in the name of philanthropy, is only a subtle attempt to assert control over the recipients. But now, all the foreign-aid funding, is additional federal deficit-spending. We ask the question, "Who is bank-rolling all this neurotic American spending-spree?" Well obviously most of the borrowed money comes from the "global dogma of international mega wealthy tycoon thug exponents" who empower financial transactions of the USA federal-reserve; and that are intent

3

on controlling the world economy at a great national loss. The ultimate motive of these crooks is to sink the US economy so they can dominate their own dastardly global supremacy under their "new world order". These hooligans are master-minds at creating crisis so they can further intervene for their own benefit; and they know the dollar must be obliterated, as the epitomized global-standard of currency-value, before the mechanized global-trade accounting-system can come into fruition. These same thugs have set up global entities like the "International Monetary Fund" that render a feeble-farce to rescue insolvent government currencies, but are actually gradual adroitness of abrupt bondage.

Industrialized out-sourcing is a favorite tactic to sabotage the USA financial system. If most everything worth trading, is manufactured in foreign countries, then there is no further remedy to correct America's trade deficit. And so now the USA deficit-spending sums a national-debt that exceeds the national GDP and has consequently robbed America's heritage for generations to come.

Email: FortunateSoldier@gmail.com
Sponsorships: https://www.paypal.com
Account# JDSRTX@juno.com

Chapter 1
TexasNationalGangstersInc
Inscribed 04/07/2011 by San JDJesuitas

The second annual board meeting was called to order by the TexasNationalGangstersInc Chairman San Jesuitas on April 5th, 2010 at 7pm with a moment of silence, in reverence to the sovereignty and grace of God, and Texas Nationalism. As the gangsters were presented, most were accompanied by their delightful and lovely ladies and all were of sound body and mind. The mindset of the Almighty God settled upon them while the roster was abdicated by the gangster Secretary San Mario.

As the meeting took course in casual conversation, the rhetoric was humorous but yet practical as the gangsters decided unanimously to establish a non-violent position within the Texas National Homeland but yet still be able to effectively achieve all resolutions. Gangsters San Ernesto and San Roberto said that the plan was originally to establish an "open and closed book" styled non-profit small private gang on behalf of Texas National Security. Then by publishing all resolutions in a reverse propaganda styled format, it will be easy enough to solicit and/or recruit criminals as auxiliary forces under command.

The ultimate motives will be to get a handle on, and to expose the underworld of illicit narcotics trafficking right here in our own back yards. Gangster Vice-chairman San Glenn agreed that will be achieved easily enough once we're on the inside, since we will then be more capable of a true reformation in Texas. Obviously, it will become

increasingly realistic, once we are from within, to gain access without violence, thru cooperative efforts, to all the illicit drugs, undocumented weapons and laundered money, located within the Texas National Boundaries. The decisive objective is to take the violence away from our own neighborhoods and borders and send it back to Columbia//Peru where it originates. It then became further resolved as the gangster Treasurer San Alfonso declared that the only way to insure such paranormal-feats is indeed by publishing all resolute intentions in a reverse-propaganda styled format.

The gangster Secretary San Mario asked what would be done with all the resources and influence that will be readily available. Gangster Chairman San Jesuitas retorted that we will get back to the discussion of those topics later but there is no doubt that everything will be done decently and in order as all progress is published. Gangsters San Andrew and San Noël suggested that the first start up program should be to establish a special infantry militia, not a legitimate one yet, but just a denigrate-militia to help all them Texas boys get a handle on the narcotics trafficking epidemic. This would be a tremendous help to the causes of needy folks throughout the Texas and Mexico region that have actually become victims of their own illicit behavior and ill created circumstance. It was then suggested by gangsters San Oscar and San Ramiro with unanimous consent to not use armaments for now until we officially declare war on illicit narcotics trafficking within our Texas national boundaries. Obviously, the gangster's resolutions can be first instigated more efficiently by means of reverse propaganda rather than by means of violence and then the best of artillery and intelligence will become further available and provided to the mercenaries assigned to the specified tasks.

—

The gangsters met at the Los Compadres Restaurant, located on the Mexican border; and the house served appetizing homemade chips & salsa, followed by a Fajita Nacho Supreme delicacy dinner platter. Beverages were ordered individually as desired; and the entertainment was kindly hosted by the restaurant owner, who has recently acquired the newest state of the art computerized sound equipment, with an unlimited song selection available. Gangsters San Joe and San Jimmy told him we sure did appreciate him putting up with a bunch of gangsters like us, and if there's anything he ever needs, just snap your finger.

The floor was engaged all evening while delightful couples tangoed throughout most of the song performances. Most folks would have thought they were just in another lime-lit dinner-club with non-stop leisure. The cost of admission was $100 per couple which covered all cost of food, beverage and entertainment. All monies was received by the gangster Treasury San Alfonso and the surplus funds was combined into the general-fund accounting to be used towards the cost of incorporating and also for further publications. Anybody who was unable to pay the entire admission fee was subsidized from the treasury.

There was no further debate because all the gangsters were of the mindset of their Lord and Savior Jesus Christ deciding that the best way to achieve such exploits is to hire the adversary's mercenaries, to defect and start from the inside. Getting back to the subject of how to use the newly and readily acquired resources and influence; it takes funding, to hire mercenaries, to eradicate the cocaine production flowing out of Columbia and Peru. The only way to get rid of the problem is to get rid of the source and that may require the annihilation of the entire Colombian

—

7

and Peruvian government and military. Vice-chairman
San Glenn reassured all the gangsters, "It's not all that
hard to do, and if we have to, we may just do it ourselves."

Chapter 2
A NATION IS BORN AGAIN
Inscribed Jan '09 by: San JDJesuitas

A soft landing theory for our USA economy was the
prelude to a series of repulsive USA presidential tactic.
The president of the USA has authority during war to
institute economic and even monetary changes. If there is
a global military force then shouldn't there be a global
currency to pay the troops and also to balance the federal
USA budget (deficit)? That equates to instant global
devaluation of the USA dollar value. Babylon is falling
and prime time is ticking away.

When we consider the whole matter, everything our
politicians say has a subliminal meaning. But there is a
better solution to the USA national security and economic
disaster that is looming on the horizon; and with much
better tactics than to merge our national sovereignty to the
United Nations in Europe. Take a map of the USA, Mexico
and Cuba; apply a protractor to the city of San Benito,
Texas and pull out a 1000 (thousand) mile radius; draw a
circle, count the states and declare sovereignty. Quality
time in Texas is to supersede from the USA Feds, because
we have now been federalized belatedly, and to excessive
disproportions.

There are still 50 (fifty) states just like it was before in the
USA, except we are just rearranged a little to reestablish
true Texas national sovereignty. Can you imagine how a
circular shaped nation like the new Texas boundaries will

—

appear on the map? The new federation will include 14 states from the former USA, 31 states in Mexico (that includes all of Mexico, excluding Baja), 4 states in Central America and cuts Cuba in half. There is still national security, sovereignty of nations, solvency, wealth, liberty and the American dream in these Middle-American states of Texas.

Never bow down to globalization. Does anybody have the courage to take the lead? There is ample support from scores of tangible forces, but there is no "Comandante en Jefe" to outline the policies. This creates a huge power vacuum in Texas. Is there anybody who can rally the forces? We need a new super-power now. Will anybody rise up to the occasion? When the task seems to be over-whelming, then take it to bay. Prematurely can sometimes be destructive; but a timely fashion will sustain stamina, to take it to task, while the Lord is on our side.

Tariffs, consumption and excise taxes can be steadily reduced, in Texas, through efficiency and by conservation. Treasury deposits will revert Texas national currency values as Texas national security further entices ethical investments and distract racketeering. Dry bones with new flesh are better than ashes to ashes and dust to dust. With new life there is new money. The gold-silver standard is most stable, non-denigrate monetary substance. Ministrant revenue is assessment seizures of racketeer assets and includes every drug lord in Columbia and Peru South America. That may also include most of the former Mexican elect and some right here in Texas also. We all know who owns what and how they acquired it. Coins of matter-factor and paper notes are of equal value if backed by treasury deposits. Purchasing power depends on the Texas international dollar-value. Texas nationally assessed industries of energy resources, transportation services, agricultural & pharmaceutical efforts, with restructured Texas national security, will virtually eliminate all need for an "Internal Revenue Service" in Texas. Most property taxes can be replaced with diminutive consumption taxes. The USA national deficit and international debts must be redistributed to specific liabilities within the representatives' individual districts and then the trade-deficits and prorated delinquency can be furthered compared to equity or solvency. Fortunately, a re-organized merger of economies, cultures and segregations is still a nation of immigrants; so the more things change the more things still stay the same.

Chapter 3
CAN TEXAS NATIONALISM
MAKE A PEACE TREATY WITH JIHAD?
Inscribed November 2009 by: San JDJesuitas

Have you ever wondered why Venezuela and Cuba does not have the continuous threat of international terrorist attacks within their homelands? First and foremost they don't allow foreigners to privately infiltrate their economy without rigidly monitored restrictions. Hence, they don't meddle in foreign affairs that don't directly concern the sovereignty of their own economy. They don't try to intimidate or circumvent the rag-heads' resources and so the rag-heads don't bother them either. Customarily, the Hispanic culture doesn't try to police the world on every extorted allegation of human-rights violations. Ensuing, they don't have the threat of commercial aircraft sabotage and terrorist attacks. Whoever coined the phrase, "human-rights" must have been either a liberal-republican or a conservative-democrat; there's not any difference.

Ironically, we have ample oil & gas resources within the USA national jurisdictions. There's enough crude oil right here within

10

the Texas regions, and Mexican Gulf to sustain all our needs. Tariffs on foreign imported mid-eastern fuel subsidies can encourage reliance upon alternative western energy resources and will also curtail our endemic consumption. Virtually, all monetary substance in a communist country is nationalized to maintain national sovereignty. The government owns the energy resources, the transportation services, as well as the agriculture and medical industries. Since their government owns all their own energy resources they are not dependent upon foreign nations to subsidize their fuel supplies.

But incredibly enough, environmentalist "tree hugging" lobbyist within the US congress have subtly imposed aura law restrictions upon the capacity of our own crude oil production & refineries. At great cost to national security we are prevented by our own lawmakers from using our own natural resources. Consequently, the USA becomes even more dependent upon the global price of fuel. The lobbyist claim that crude oil production & refineries are more harmful to their environment; whereas it is far more harmful to be dependent upon our enemy's fuel supplies than it is to use our own natural resources. These constraints were ushered in unawares on Gore's watch as Al Gore is the greatest stooge of all time tree hugging. Incongruously, the Chinese are drilling for oil just 50 miles off the USA coastline without our regimen imposed upon them.

The USA has become increasingly dependent upon Mid-eastern oil supplies, with spiraling constrictions, thus greatly empowering our avowed enemies. Referendums would be futile efforts as US fat-cat politicians become filthy rich with kickbacks, underhanded payoffs, and contracts awarded without competitive bidding. Obviously, the wars in Iraq are direct results of the lustful American political rapacity. We can stick our heads in the sand and remain in denial, but inconspicuously, our elected big-shot Republicans have concealed their extensive control over the global price of oil. How can gasoline prices

---

11

drop substantially just a few weeks (it happens every time) before elections? Go figure, we've been hoodwinked again as our selected rulers betray our American sovereignty and at great expense of the USA national security. But fortunately there are resolutions, by proposing a Texas National peace treaty, prevaricating threats of international terrorism within our Texas National region.

Everybody knows, so it would be absurd to go about seriously trying to prove that foreign politics is more corrupt than that in the USA. Moreover, we would cringe with dismay if we knew what really goes on behind the scenes. Why did the FBI suddenly vacate the federal building in OK City on the day of the bombing, but neglect to evacuate all the occupants? The USA secret services could have also prevented the 911 catastrophe as they were aware of the preceding and forthcoming threats. Languorously, we almost conclude to believe that the USA intelligence allowed the 911 bombings to deploy a more malignant stimulus. Once again the FBI vacated the twin towers on the day of the disasters and imprudently abandoned the multitudes to perish. Perchance the CIA needed a more politically correct global precedent for another Iraq invasion. Americans have always, in the past, been swift to impose economic embargoes against weaker nations that won't conform

to their vogue.   But now with the diminishing USA dollar value, Americans are suddenly realize great repercussions. The mid-eastern nations want us out of their countries now. Instead of imposing embargoes, even worse, the turn-about against us is our dependency on their petroleum resources, and at extremely extorted global prices. Sequentially, the backlash has provoked intense and rancorous hatred from brutal and perilous, USA enemies. In return, the double faced Russians and Chinese have formed stalwart alliances with most USA opposition. Hence, the sole USA allies are the Brits, virtually leaving the Americans alone, as always, to enforce their own resolutions. But Hugo Chavez still sells gasoline in Venezuela for .12 cents; and he also subsidizes the food and medical cost for his citizens, with revenue from his state-owned energy resources.

Inevitably, there are radical political changes about to occur in Cuba also. Before Castro croaks, I must, try to again, go tell him about Jesus. We all know that he's been a tyrant, but the good Lord can still open his spiritually blinded eyes and save his eternal soul from a devil's hell. The scripture says: "God is not willing that any should perish but that all would come to repentance". Christianity has only misunderstandings, not disagreements. Nevertheless, when Castro expires, the chain of command transfers to Fidel's brother, who is not much younger. Raul Castro is still top dog general of the Cuban military forces. Unfortunately, without an intrepid Texas National Alliance, he may lack the necessary charisma to maintain authority as commander in chief of Cuba. But before this phenomenon occurs, now is the developing time to cajole Fidel with beneficial propositions. Sometime it becomes congruous, although despising the character of the gentry, to emulate their conventionality and adapt your self to its humors, until such a time as they can be converted; in which case virtuous conduct would only prejudice you, but well-being could be more obtainable by following the course of opposition. So by considering the whole matter we conclude that there may be a course that appears to be eccentric, by which safety is secured; whereas a line of conduct having the appearance of virtue, which to follow would be ruinous.

Moreover, in route again to Cuba, and making resolute

announcements prior to arrival, it will be a pre-requisite to swing by Mexico City and slap Felipe in the face with our new Texas National map & money.

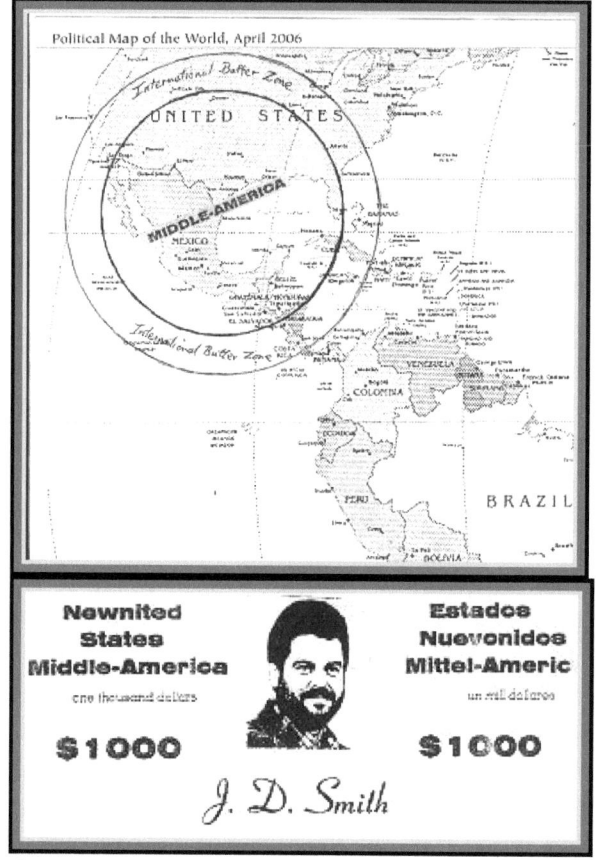

Accordingly, we must further guarantee immediate withdrawals to all capital investment claims within their innate territories. Then we must simultaneously "NATIONALIZE" without hesitation, all Arabic owned assets within our Texas National borders, further equating the confiscations as "even score"; whereupon, intense censorship of all rag-head Muslims remaining within our borders will expedite their deportation, detention or fundamental rectification. Fortunately, we still have tolerance, acceptance and freedom under Texas Nationalism because the camel-jockeys remaining within Texas' jurisdictions must still have three choices: 1) Return back to their homeland.

2) Pledge allegiance to the Texas National flag and work for food, shelter and safety. 3) Hard labor in Texas Prisons.

Returning to the question now of whether or not Texas Nationalism can make a peace treaty with the sand-niggers; the best peace treaty we can negotiate with any Muslim country is for Texas to gladly give up George Bush's whereabouts; and then pledge to refrain from any further involvement into their intrinsic affairs. They don't have a single solitary thing that resembles anything we might possibly need, or even come close to anything we want; so if leave us alone, we leave them alone, is much better than the alternative of lighting up their homeland like a glass-bottom glowing-bowel for the next 1000 years. Sardonically, the Venezuelan and Cuban governments adjudicate superbly with the Arabs, and so can we.
Golden Rule #1--Don't wake sleeping dogs; #2-- Don't start a fight you can't finish; #3--Don't bully people who aren't harassing you first. But please send the bounty hunters to get San JDJesuitas busted-out and back home if he gets in a jam.

Such stratagem will also squelch the conflicts between the opposing Mafia and the Mexican government rivalries by allurement of Mexican dominion in a new Middle-American federation under Texas Nationalism. So ensuing, the short-cut returning home to Texas will be prime time to patronize Venezuela with a visit, to congenially flatter Hugo for being such a grand philanthropist statesman, and further subsidizing gasoline fuel-prices to his constituency at below-cost.

Chapter 4
CRUELTY AND CLEMENCY
LOVE OR FEAR
Ascribed 04/28/2010 by: San JDJesuitas

An Autocrat should desire to be accounted merciful and not cruel, but he should be careful not to abuse this tactful quality of mercy. Moreover, newly acquired regional jurisdictions, above all others, are impossible to escape a name for cruelty, since new States are full of dangers. Therefore, the Autocracy should therefore disregard the reproach of cruelty where it enables him to keep his subjects faithfully united because he who quells disorder by a very few examples will in the end be more merciful than he, who, to avoid the imputation of cruelty, suffers suffers a society to be torn to pieces by factions. So if we look at things in their true light, it will be seen that what might seem to be the cruelty of an Autocracy, is in reality far more merciful than excessive leniency, which suffers things to take their own course and so result in rapine and bloodshed; for these hurt the entire State, whereas the severities of the Autocracy injure individuals only.

And here comes the question whether it is better to be loved rather than feared or feared rather than loved. It might be answered that we should wish to be both, but since love and fear can hardly exist together, if we must choose between them, it is safer to be feared than loved. For of men it may generally be affirmed that they are thankless, fickle, false, studious to avoid danger, greedy of gain, devoted to you while you confer benefits upon them, and ready while the need is remote, to shed blood and sacrifice their property, their lives, and their children for you; but when it comes near they turn against you.

An Autocrat, therefore, who without otherwise securing himself, who builds wholly on their professions, is undone. For the friendships we buy with a price, and do not gain by greatness and nobility of character, though fairly earned are not made good but fail when we need them the most. Moreover, men are less careful how they offend him who makes himself loved than him who makes himself feared. For love is held by the tie of obligation, which, because men are a sorry breed; is broken on every prompting of self-interest. But fear, is bound by the apprehension of punishment, which never looses its grasp.

Nevertheless, his perspicacity should not be to ready of belief, nor too easily set in motion; nor be the first to raise alarms; but should temper prudence with kindness so that too great a confidence in others shall not throw him off his guard, nor unwarranted distrust render himself insupportable. An Autocrat should therefore inspire fear in such wise that if he does not win love he may escape hate. For a man may very well be feared and yet not hated, as will always be the case so long as he does not intermeddle with the property or with the women of his citizens and subjects. And if constrained to put anyone to death, he should do so only when there is manifest cause or reasonable justification. But, above all, he must abstain from the rightful possessions of others. For men will sooner forget the death of their father than the loss of their patrimony. Moreover, if pretext for confiscation are never to seek, then reasons for shedding blood are fewer and sooner exhausted; because he who has once begun to live by rapine always finds reasons for taking what is not his. But when an Autocrat is with his army, and his soldiers under his command, he must entirely disregard the reproach of cruelty, for without such a reputation in its Captain, no army can be held together or kept ready for emergency.

Returning now to the question of being loved or feared, We all know, that since his being loved depends upon his subjects, while his being feared depends upon himself, even when it gets lonely at the top, a wise Autocrat should build upon what is his own, and not on what rests with others. Only he must always do his best to escape hatred.

Chapter 5
NOBEL CAUSES
Ascribed 4/30/10 by San JDJesuitas

About 40yrs ago the US government removed the ten
commandments of Moses from where it was displayed
On the wall of the US Supreme Court. Then they began
to teach Darwinism and the theory of evolution to children
in school instead of teaching the Biblical truths of how God
designed and created the entire universe. Since then it has
become politically incorrect to even voice public prayers,
in US Congress, in the name of Jesus because we have
allowed foreign theologies to infiltrate our government
and society. Hence, our compromise for the prevalence of
equality, and our efforts to be all things to all people has
become of greater status than the vitality of the Christian
faith on which this nation hinges and was founded upon.
So now we are mandated to tread softly so as not to offend
any opposing anti-Christian faiths in the USA, and to not
publicly pray nor to proclaim our faith in the Lord Jesus
Christ, because it may offend some American pagans.

Ironically enough, the USA government will soon
resemble those of impoverished third world nations.
The USA national debt has now completely sold-out the
heritage of their grandchildren and has already been
bought-out and now mostly owned by under-handed
capitalist despots, and ruthless foreign governments.
This demise within our USA society is the result from
how the USA has turned their back on God and is no
longer truly a Christian nation. As a result, the greatest
global threat now is that the USA will soon become an
uninhabitable wasteland, as they are utterly over-thrown

—

by their enemies, and violated without mercy by the heathen nations that George Bush sullied for a decade.

Unfortunately, there is no longer a truly democratic government in the USA, but America became an unconstitutional hierarchy when George Bush and his Brother, Jeb Bush, thwarted the democratic electoral process in Florida in the year 2000 USA presidential election. George Bush Jr. did not legally win the US presidency neither with a majority of the popular vote nor with a sufficient electoral-college vote, but to the contrary in the year 2000 the US presidential election, by all rights belonged to his contender. Unfortunately, since Jeb Bush was governor of Florida at that time he was able to render the vote count there fraudulent by an electronic voting mob-styled recount that was never certified. Hence the USA government became unconstitutionally non-democratic at that time and was transformed to a regime when the presidential election was thwarted by these *"THUG - BROTHERS"*.

As a result, the 911 catastrophes would have never occured

if Bush had not been in the White House illegally.
The attack on the world trade centers was the direct result
of the rancorous hatred and vengeance against the former
George Bush Sr. administration from when he invaded
Iraq the first time during the Desert Storm. And
considering once again how the credible indication of
fore-knowledge of the 911 attacks is sufficient evidence
of his administration's circuitous involvement; evidently,
the true motives of the Gulf wars were only the result of
the lust and greed of the Bush dynasty for their own
personal gain, thru their ability to control the mid-eastern
oil reserves.

Sorry to say, but Bush intentionally ignored the housing
market crisis and is responsible for the collapse of our USA
economy. It was in the news for a year before it happened.
So as you make an informed decision for yourself you can
weep as you read the archives that were published weekly
in the USA-Today newspaper, with top economic experts
warning about the approaching economic devastation.
The economic melt-down could have been prevented in
2008, before it happened, with executive orders to freeze
all the sub-prime home-financing adjustable interest rates
and to prevent the unjustified payment increases, thus
preventing millions of home foreclosures that caused
domino-effects of economic ruin in the USA. But now
George Bush has made claims in his recent interviews how
he was blind-sided by the disastrous unfolding economic
events on his watch. With the simple stroke of a pen from
the oval office, the president could have altered history
and turned the economic-tide upward instead of down.
But the mad-man was having too much fun playing
Machiavelli; so as usual Bush chose to endorse the fleecing
of Americans once more, and continued to pad the pockets
of his corporate comrades again with government bailouts.

———

He was also up to his ears in the 1980's S&L scandals. Bush is corrupt with innocent blood all over himself and he is the worst thing that ever happened to the USA. Don't forget how back in 2006 Bush declares Columbia and Peru as #1 USA allied trading partners. Moreover, the Columbian president at that time, Alvaro Uribe had not fought against Revolutionary Armed Forces of Columbia and the gorillas' forces but only pacified them to give them a compensated cut of the unlawful narcotics trafficking profits. Obviously, the illicit drug trade of cocaine coming out of Colombia // Peru flowing thru Texas has not decreased but to the contrary has only increased while Bush was in office. The former Bush administration was involved up to their nostrils also because obviously they have ample intelligence, and can continually observe the truth with global-satellite observation. So even worse than the Bush dynasty's lust and greed for personal gain from control of the mid-eastern foreign oil reserves, his greed for personal gain from illicit narcotics trafficking is far more intolerable to his countrymen.

The whole world knows it, but the capitalist still refuse to acknowledge all the disaster and debt Bush has brought upon Americans with his daddy's personal vendetta Gulf war? The USA is going down for the final time and this time they are not going to rise back up again. One thing for certain is that Americans must never raise a hand against Bush but nobody is impermeable as he has been taught to believe, and what goes around comes around. They claim to be Texas natives but they're only dreaming and they have no legal rights whatsoever here since Jr. was born in Connecticut and his daddy was born in Maine. They live in Houston and in Dallas; but we do not have to protect them when their enemies come to take them away. Unfortunately, they can never obtain exile here in Texas

—

because Texas National Security will soon come to an all time low as long as George Bush and his daddy are given refuge here. They have both arrogantly accumulated a delinquency of excessive enemies that would gladly destroy this entire region just to get their scalp; *(motivating all advocates of his protective custody and also those who would see him jailed)* to stuff his incarcerated happy-ass along with his best buddy Alvaro, the former Columbia President, into exile at the bottom of Dyer-Straights and keep them there until hell freezes over.

A democratic government can no longer survive when the people become too ungodly to rule themselves. This is when a dictatorial regime will rise up to power in the USA and such is exactly what is unfolding now under the current administration. Since the USA has now become nothing more than a police-state, and is approaching a despotic regimen, if we are going to comply with any such changes under a degenerate USA globalization, then we will be better off in Texas to succeed from the USA federal union and become our own independent nation right here once again under our own Texas national heritage.
A wise man one said, "Give me liberty or give me death"; and now the time has arrived to separate men from boys. So to the contrary, when people who rule are righteous, then there is no doubt that a Christian theology of communism in Texas will actually be the best form of government, to ascribe equal opportunity to all citizens.

We all hate to realize the stark truth but we all know all those Jihad Muslim folks over there in the mid-east, who George Bush repeatedly violated, are not going to ever forget or forgive the USA under any circumstance. Our greatest fear should be that they will eventually find a way to utterly destroy this country; and the destruction of

America could very well happen under the current USA administration, whose current leadership does not originate in the western hemisphere. Terrorism rages unchecked, and international piracy is the norm in Indonesia and in Kenya where his roots remain. We already know, because the man has already stated, that when the political winds of change come, he will return back to his Islamic roots; so don't be foolish enough to ever believe he will try to protect Americans. Let's just hope and pray that we can keep the devastative fallout away from the boundaries of our Texas National Homeland.

Hence, we are going to need an alternative regimen of interim government at that time here in Texas because the so called democracy here in the USA will become total anarchy. A new alternative Christian communist regime will then have to be instituted straight away under Texas nationalism and with Christianity as our Texas national faith. It is not to be expected that many people will totally agree with a Christian communist philosophy, as most folks in the western world have obviously been taught that communism is not decent. Nevertheless, Communist China, has become the most powerful and successful economic super-power in the world. Contrary to popular American opinion, there is nothing about the theory of a communist government that has ever mandated atheism, but instead the atheistic environment that was imposed within the Soviet Union was due only to the ungodly rulers that governed at that time. Fortunately, on behalf of our Texas national Security, we can and will expel any and all creeds, at that time, from our Texas National borders, that dares to voice any opposition to a new "Theological Christian Communism", under the independent flag of TEXAS Nationalism. Theoretically, a communist government is a system of social organization based on the holding of all property in common. Actual ownership of all property is ascribed to the community as a whole or to the state with an economic system characterized by collective ownership of property. The organization of labor is also for a common advantage of all members, because communism is a system of government in which the state plans and controls the economy; and where a single authoritarian party, often holds authority, further asserting progress toward a higher social order, where citizenship shares resources equally.

CHAPTER 6
BABYLON IS FALLING
AND PRIME TIME IS TICKING AWAY
Ascribed on 08/01/2011 by San JDJesuitas

Now San JDJesuitas was the eldest among his brethren, and was also the heir to six generations of his native TEXAS national birth-right. Moreover, he was a man of modern-day times, who nonetheless was tutored from his youth to be practical, with old-fashion values in all of his dealings; and to work cleverly with his hands, to never become unsettled by political correctness, and to always remain original. Therefore, customary society would occasionally deem him unsociable or censured of mainstream, because aside from all endorsement, he would never kneel to mortal mankind. Hence by any means even till now, he freely serves only his creator, and thus regards the LORD his God alone.

And when Jesuitas was grown, he went out unto the brethren of his homeland, contemplating upon the plight of their social disintegration. And he observed that all the elders of TEXAS were greatly distressed with all their endurance, as realization of their bankrupt destiny became overwhelming. They knew their offspring would soon be enslaved in bondage, because it was obvious to everybody, that Babylon was crumpling, and that prime time was quickly slipping away in the USA. And lifting up their voice in one accord, they wept bitterly within their spirit, until they had no more strength to suppurate.

Suddenly there was a clamor of all those who were likeminded of Jesuitas, as they acknowledge how the contravention from Columbia and Peru, has raked America's offspring over the coals, by supplying them with illicit narcotics, and that has turn out to be lethal addictions. And the chorus of reproach was set in somber judgment, as the voice of their contrition was heard from heaven above, even unto the throne of the LORD God; and He was further inclined to attend unto their outcry. Then Jesuitas earnestly sought after elucidation, and he opened his bible to read from the Holy Scriptures. And by taking heed to God's holy word accordingly, Jesuitas cleansed himself in all of his ways. It was so then, that by faith, he received the willpower to purge his mind and heart from all unrighteousness. And as he sought after grace from God, he found favor in the eyes of his creator. Then meditating upon the scripture, he enquired towards a disclosure of wisdom from the LORD.

Now the obvious and immediate danger is that the USA national defense is despondent without virtuous leadership; and America is off-guard with complacency. Thus, there are giants in the land, averring of one accord, that are to strong to subdue! So reading accordingly, from the book of Judges, Jesuitas focused intently upon the instruction, of which therein described the unfolding of an unbridled retribution of Gideon in Manasseh. And then being led by the Holy Spirit of discernment, he inscribed the words that were perceived within his intuitive sagacity. And Jesuitas revealed a feat of unrestrained vengeance that soon will be set in motion.

There is a tremendous accumulated wealth in Columbia and Peru and these valuable and abundant resources must be sequestered by our own hired-guns. The spoils of war must be brought all the way back home to Texas through Mexico, to pay restitution for illicit narcotics trafficking, and to squelch the social decline that is now being inflicted upon innocent people by the rage of civil war in Mexico.

No doubt, this incentive will incite and stimulate an aggravated Texas National Independent invasion in the "no man's land", on behalf of Texas National Sovereignty and Security. Alien investors, who have no legal right there, continually excavate the most valuable supply of pure gold in Peru, and the clearest diamonds, rubies, emeralds and all manner of precious stones are found abundantly in Columbia. As a result, it will also become vital to raze the entire government and military forces there in those same South American countries. Now, more than ever before, they grow the coca-leaf cash-crop for the black-market in Peru, but the natives who have lived there for centuries, still suffer immensely from malnutrition. Incongruously, some hokey gay-lord Canadian hoodwinks obtained exclusive access to all the gold mines, under the table, from blood-spattered Peruvian crooks that control the government resources there, and where tons of pure gold is being extracted continually from the gold-mines within the Andes Mountains in Peru. Nonetheless, the inhabitants, who have lived there for centuries, receive no royalty entitlement benefits whatsoever, from the immense wealth, but only get an eroded and toxic environment that polluted from the gold-mining engender.

And when those who were with Jesuitas read the words that had conveyed unreservedly from his demeanor, all the lexis of true hope was proliferating quickly. As a result, the rightful benefactors, within the national boundaries of Texas, encouraged themselves in the God of Abraham, Isaac & Jacob; the LORD Jesus Christ is his almighty name. Then the spirit of the LORD descended among the congregation of the righteous, further impressing a forayed incursion of the enemy fortresses.

And so they resolved with great confidence, to ploy a pursuit and recovery of all losses and they sought after the imminence of divine insight, to eradicate the poisonous sources, which are flowing northward continually, from the illicit narcotics producing countries. Then those who were of one accord with Jesuitas, became even more quicken than all antediluvian, and declared, "Let us now turn the tide of devastation aside and backwards as we further persuade the Mexican cartel, that it is indeed more profitable now, to sever the illicit narcotics trafficking at the source of origin, and to further seize all the wealth at the place of derivation." Henceforth, according to God's word, they all further tacit, to rest by faith in the LORD,

---

and to not grow weary or faint within their spirit.
Then in sequence, they rose up early the next morning,
with renewed spiritual strength, and of mighty resolution.

All of a sudden, the chattering rumor of a dissident
invasion increase quickly, and terror struck like a plague
in the heart of the enemy forces of the illicit drug-lords
and narcotics producers. So as the Columbians and the
Peruvians, and all the children of the illicit narcotics
traffickers, lay along the valley like grasshoppers for huge
number, their forces were unaccountable, and as the sand
by the sea side for multitude. And as Jesuitas disguised
himself and arrived at the quarries with his a spies, behold,
there was a man that told dream unto his fellow and said,
"Behold, I dreamed a dream, and lo, a cake of barley bread
tumbled into the host of the cocaine producers, and came
unto a tent, and smote it that it fell, and overturned it, that
the tent lay along." And his fellow answered in great fear
and said, "This is nothing else save the defensive resilience
of a most tactical foil, which is now forthcoming of the
pervasive Texas National Independence movement;
namely one man, i.e. San JDJesuitas, the native son and
benefactor of Texas National heritage, who is now forced
to wage retribution. For now the LORD his God, for His
own name's sake, hath delivered his enemies and their
entire host into his hand."

And it was so, when Jesuitas heard the telling of the
dream, and the interpretation thereof, that he worshipped
the LORD his God, and returned unto the elders of his
homeland in Texas, and said, "Arise and be of good cheer!
The LORD our God hath now delivered into our hand,
to subdue the host of all the illicit narcotics trafficking
heathen, and to further seize all their wealth, to repay
our honest debts to all mankind." Moreover, we shall

now incite the pursuit and obliteration of our enemy, and shall indeed recover all losses; for the LORD Jesus Christ our God reigns in the homeland of Texas, and our heritage will soon be debt-free again!

So let us turn about now to be faultless, always encouraging ourselves in the LORD our God, and running the race with endurance. Rejoice continually now with assurance and thanksgiving, because the legatee of Texas National Independence will never be sold into bondage, even until that great and terrible day of the Lord, which will come as a thief in the night; in which the heavens shall pass away with a great noise, and the elements shall melt with fervent heat, and the earth also and the works that are therein shall be burned up. Blessed are they which are called unto the marriage supper of the Lamb. These sayings are faithful and true: and the Lord God of the holy prophets sent his angel to show unto his servants the things which must shortly be done. Blessed and holy is he that hath part in the first resurrection: on such the second death hath no power, but they shall be priests of God; reigning this entire world, a thousand years with Christ.

Chapter 7
PRINCIPLES OF COMMERCE
Ascribed 04/29/2010 by: San JDJesuitas

A rich country, in the same manner as a rich man, is supposed to be a country abounding in money; and to heap up gold and silver in a country is supposed to be the readiest way to enrich it. For some time after the discovery of America, the first inquiry of the Spaniards used to be, when they arrived upon an unknown coast, if there was any gold or silver to be found in the neighborhood. By the information which they received, they judged

29

whether or not the country was worth the conquering. If a nation could be separated from the entire world, it would be of no consequence how much, or how little money circulated in it. The consumable goods which were circulated by means of this money would only be exchanged for a greater or smaller number of pieces; but the real wealth or poverty of the country would depend altogether upon the abundance or scarcity of those consumable goods. It is otherwise with countries which have connections with foreign nations, and which are obligated to carry on foreign wars, and to maintain fleets and armies abroad.

But it is not always necessary to accumulate gold and silver in order to enable a country to carry on foreign wars, and to maintain fleets and armies in distant countries. Military forces are maintained, not with gold and silver, but with consumable goods. Therefore, the nation which can obtain collaterals, from the annual produce of its domestic industry, from the revenue arising out of its lands, labors, and consumable stock, which has the wherewithal to purchase consumable goods in distant countries, can maintain foreign wars there.
So even still, a nation may purchase the pay and provisions of an army in a distant country several different ways: by sending abroad either, first, some part of its accumulated gold and silver; or secondly, some part of the annual produce of its manufactures; or last of all, some part of its annual rude produce.

Nevertheless, it would be ludicrous to go about seriously trying to prove that power and wealth does not only consist in money, or in gold and silver; but in what money purchases, and what is valuable only for purchasing. Money, no doubt, is part of the national capital but if gold and silver should at any time fall short in a country, there are expedients for supplying their place. Commodities, for that reason, regulate a market-value more easily and exactly according to where they exceed, rather than those where they fall short of effectual demand. If the materials of manufacturing are wanted, industry must stop. If provisions are wanted, the people must starve. But if money is wanted, barter will supply its place, although sometimes with a great deal of inconvenience.

Obviously, the qualities of every commodity, which human industry can either purchase or produce naturally, regulates itself in every country according to the effectual demand, or according to the demand of those who are willing to pay the whole rent, labor, and profits which must be paid in order to bring it to market. But with gold or silver, on account of the small bulk and great value of those metals, no commodity can be more easily transported from one place to another, from the places where they are cheap to those where they are dearer; from the places where they exceed, to those where they fall short of effectual demand.

Likewise, the gold and silver which can be considered as accumulated or stored up in any country may be distinguished into three parts: first, the circulating money; secondly, the money which may have been collected by many years parsimony, and laid up in the treasury; and last of all, the private resources of families. Unfortunately, in Texas, at this time, we don't have any authentic and bona-fide circulating legal-tender; only the USA paper notes that are quickly loosing their value. We have very little hard cash, at this time, laid up in the treasury; but fortunately, on behalf of Texas national sovereignty and security, the diktat still maintains rights to the subvention, by requesting access to private family resources.

Chapter 8
...IF YOU WANT WEALTH...
JESUITAS SEEKS TRUE NOBILITY OF MEXICO
Inscribed on 08/04/11 by San JDJesuitas

There is a tremendous accumulated wealth in Columbia as they continually excavate the most valuable supply there of the clearest diamonds, rubies, emeralds and all manner of precious stones. Peru also has the most accrued supply of earth's finest gold, found abundantly right there in the gold-mines of the Andes Mountains. These valuable and abundant resources must be sequestered by our own hired-guns and brought back home to Texas through Mexico to pay compensation for the harm inflicted upon innocent people, from illicit narcotics trafficking that has raged this civil war in Mexico. No doubt, this incentive will further incite and stimulate an aggravated invasion of Columbia and Peru, on behalf of Texas National Sovereignty and Security. Unfortunately it will also become vital to raze the entire government and military forces there in those South American countries.

It doesn't take much savoir-faire to determine that the desire and the reason for all narcotics trafficking throughout Mexico is to acquire wealth. Nevertheless, the acquisition of true nobility brings much more honor and satisfaction than any amount of blood-money could ever offer. When the Texas and Mexican national mercenary forces returned back to their native soil from their conquest, after the war being waged in Colombia and Peru, after having destroyed the illicit drug supplies and confiscating all the enemy's wealth and resources, then not only have these warriors acquired wealth, power and prestige towards the prosperity of their homeland, but moreover they have attained true, nobility and dignity for their own name sake.

We can rest assured that, at that time, all the mafia gang members who will help destroy the rouge government armed forces of Colombia and Peru will be in fact entitled to great benefits, of their own heritage, at that time in their mother-country; because as a result of eradicating the illicit drug traffic within their realm, they will consequently have also squelched the bloodshed and violence throughout Mexico. The Mexican federal government has good intentions of protecting their own best interest within their national boundaries but they are nevertheless incapable of true reformation because they are only linking the control of narcotics trafficking in Mexico. But obviously, the only remedy to stop cocaine trafficking throughout Mexico, is an incision, through the cocaine production, at the source of origin. And perhaps somebody should inform the narco-traffickers about how the US economy and the almighty USA $-dollar-$ is on the brink of collapse and destruction.

Without a doubt it will be much more profitable for the narco-traffickers to invade Columbia and Peru and to confiscate all the wealth because inevitably there will soon be no further profit for the Mexican drug cartels when local governments decriminalize the illicit drugs. There will then be no further benefits afforded to the narco-

—

traffickers who pursue after wealth, power and prestige. Only the righteous mercenaries who truly resolve to turn the tide of illegal drug flow aside and backward, after having severed the illicit drug flow and thus have acquired true nobility, will then truly be worthy of the royalties to further take dominion over their government in Mexico.

And now the Mexican Mafia has recently questioned how such power of nobility can be guaranteed. A wise man once said that anybody who can deduce the illicit drug epidemic in Mexico can in turn do anything they desire. Can somebody please explain why the Mafia is unable to realize they are transporting the illicit drugs in the wrong direction? The conflicts within the Mexican drug cartels are killing their own families and are further slaughtering their own good and innocent people when they should only be subjugating the enemy at the source of production. So now it has become most imperative for the TexasNationalGangsterInc to addresses the Mexican drug cartels, within their domain. These distinguished cartels include but are not limited to the Gulf Cartel, the los Zetas Cartel, the Carrillo Fuentes Organization, the la Familia Michoacana Cartel, the Sinaloa Cartel and the Beltran Levy Organization.

Now is the opportune time to come out of the darkness and into the light, so that all deeds can be made manifest. The Holy Scriptures declare: "Every soul is precious in the God's sight but He cannot look upon sinful men without atonement from the shed blood of the Lord Jesus Christ; and this atonement can only be received thru repentance." Therefore, the time is at hand to turn away from evil and to seek after redemption for the soul. We all have an eternal soul and will give an account for our own deeds whether good or evil. The scripture says that everybody must work out their own salvation with fear and trembling before the almighty God.

Consequently, we must now start driving back the devastation southward and not northward. Fortunately, these resolutions will then ultimately bring the peaceful conclusion to the civil war being waged right now between the Mexican Mafia drug cartel-rivalries that are warring against the Mexican federal army. Hence, the second annual board meeting of the TexasNationalGangsterInc was called to order, by Chairman San Jesuitas on April 5, 2011 for this reason, and the gangsters resolved unanimously that narco-trafficking is the # 1 public enemy throughout the entire Texas and Mexico region. The newly established gang in Texas, has therefore established, the #1 priority resolution, to rid their entire Texas National jurisdictions of illicit narcotics trafficking.

Everybody knows that the los Zetas Cartel were the original lineup of the most valiant and highly trained Mexican Military Special Forces, and because of their superior qualifications they were solicited and bought by means of extra lucrative offers from the Mexican Mafia forces, to desert and become the muscle of the Gulf Cartel in the 1990s. Therefore, it is further resolved that the National Gangsters of Texas must adopt the same recruiting tactics that the Mafia used when they signed-up the los Zetas Cartel. Evidently, the only way the problem will be alleviated is to eradicate and sever the illicit narcotics supply at the source of production.

Mexican president Felipe Calderon is trying to refer to cocaine trafficking within the limits of Mexico, but that task is impossible until the production of cocaine is subject to the source in Colombia and Peru. So now, a subtle dialogue will now obviously be customary between the under-world drug-lord bosses of the Mexican Mafia, and above-board accordingly, with Chairman San Jesuitas. Despite the fact that the los Zetas Cartel have evolved accordingly into an exclusive narco-trafficking force by request of their own conscription, this internal rivalry has caused a covetous conspiracy within the Gulf Cartel, the Sinaloa Cartel and the la Familia Cartel. The rivals all seem now to resent and plot together to scheme against the los Zetas Cartel; but yet they can still be reached with reasoning and gathered together on the common outright grounds to set trivial differences aside, and stop the unnecessary blood-shed between the contending drug-gangs rivals, who are also warring against the Mexican federal military. These very same drug-cartel offenders must now evolve between all gang members of Mexican drug cartels, as united-mercenary auxiliary-forces under command against Colombia and Peru, to wipe-out the government military forces throughout that entire region.

Therefore, the TexasNationalGangstersInc are indeed pleased to declare that Chairman San Jesuitas is able and willing to provide the inside information and intelligence necessary as to pin-point the exact locations of the most valuable resources in Columbia and Peru that will be necessary not only to finance the exuberant costs of war but to further instigate and galvanize the proposed invasions also. Accordingly, as it has been resolved to invade and obliterate the entire government military force in Columbia and Peru, as a result all the Mexican drug cartels will therefore be sought after and enticed with lucrative offers to further help provide the muscle necessary to seize and transport the spoils-of-war back home all the way through Mexico to Texas. These valuable resources must then be further used to rectify the damage, inflicted on innocent victims of illicit narcotic production that is currently being conveyed from Columbia and Peru through the Mexico and Texas corridors, back home to the USA black-market consumers. This corruption is currently causing intense blood-shed throughout the entire Texas and Mexico region.

Moreover, we all know the Mexican Mafia narco-trafficking forces have ample recruits and fire-power, if they choose to subdue this evil force of poison flowing northward from no-man's-land. Texas has the intelligence to pin-point the precise positions of the enemy's resources, wealth and assets and there is also plenty of man-power, fire-power and resources available in Texas to locate and destroy the exact locations of the narcotics production. The entire rouge government military must be razed in those same wayward countries, as all the gold, silver and precious stones are further sequestered and conveyed back to Mexico and Texas, to reimburse our creditors here for the extreme cost of war, and also for the exuberant cost related to the smothering of illicit narcotics production.

Obviously there are ample forces and resources available to quickly and easily defeat this enemy, but Mexico currently has no commander in chief to outline policies. So let the true nobility of Mexico be known unto all, as they rise up now with the TexasnationalGanstersInc. Embracing and assuming these resolutions, will turn the tide of devastation aside and backwards, and will bring peace and prosperity once again to the Mexican homeland.

Chapter 9
THE USE OF SPIES
Ascribed 04/30/2010 by: San JDJesuitas

Although according to estimates, the soldiers of the enemy exceed ours in number, but that shall advantage them nothing in the matter of victory. Therefore we shall declare now that victory can be achieved. Although the enemy be stronger in numbers, we may prevent them from fighting, further scheming so as to discover their plans and the likelihood of their success. If we rouse them and learn the principle of their activity or inactivity we can force them to reveal themselves, so as to find out their vulnerable spots. Then carefully comparing the opposing forces with our own, we may discover where strength is superabundant and where it is deficient. In making those tactical dispositions, the highest pitch we can attain is to reveal them now.

Concealing our dispositions would be unsafe from the mediocre prying of the subtlest spies, who can easily be converted right now to become our own machinations of the most astute brains. Spies cannot be properly managed without benevolence and candor. None should be more liberally rewarded and in no other business should greater confidentiality be preserved. They cannot be gainfully engaged unless regarded with refined intuitive sagacity. Without subtle ingenuity of mind, one cannot determine for certain if their reports are truthful. If a secret piece of news is divulged by a spy before the time is developed, they must be given punitive and merciless partition, without exceptions, together with all to whom the secret was told.

How victories are produced out of the enemy's own tactics is what multitudes cannot comprehend. All men can see the tactics of conquest, but what non can see is the strategy out of which victory evolves.

Equation 1-1994

Do not repeat the tactics which have gained one victory, but let the methods be regulated by the infinite variety of circumstances.

What enables the wise sovereign and the good commander to strike and conquer, and achieve feats beyond the reach of ordinary men, is foreknowledge. However, this foreknowledge cannot be obtained inductively from experience, nor can it be elicited from spirits, or by any deductive calculation. Knowledge of the enemy's disposition can only be obtained from other men. Therefore the subordination of spies is preferential, of whom there are five classes: 1) local spies; 2) inward spies; 3) converted spies; 4) doomed spies; 5) surviving spies. When these five kinds of spy are at work, none can discover the secret system. This is called *"divine manipulation of the threads"*. It is the sovereign's most precious faculty. Having local-spies will employ the services of the inhabitants of a district. Having inward-spies will make use of officials of the enemy. Having converted-spies will manage the enemy's spies and use them for our own purpose. Having doomed-spies means doing certain things openly for purpose of deception, and allowing our spies to know of them and report them to the enemy. Surviving-spies, finally, are those who bring back news from the enemy's camp. Hence it is that which none in the whole army, are relations to be more intimately maintained, than with spies.

Be utmost subtle at all times and use your spies for every kind of business. The enemy's emissaries, who have come to spy, must be sought out and enticed with rewarding bribes, and seduced with lucrative leisure. They must be scrumptiously dined, to then be led away and comfortably housed. Hence, they will become converted spies and available for our services.

It is through the information brought by the converted spy that we are able to acquire and employ local and inward space owing to his information; again, that we can cause the doomed spy to carry false tidings to the enemy. And lastly, by his information, the surviving spy can be used on appointed occasions. So spying in all five varieties is to acquire knowledge of the enemy; and this knowledge can most accurately be derived, in the first instance from the converted spy. Hence, it is always most essential that the converted spy be treated with utmost liberality.
So as for now, while there is still an outward facade of freedom in Texas, let us never neglect to tell friend & foe alike about the saving grace of the LORD Jesus Christ; and then proceed quickly with whatever is necessary, to retain our Texas national security.

Chapter 10
THE BUCK $TOPS IN TEXAS
Inscribed Jan. 2008 by: San JDJesuitas

THERE'S GOOD NEWS AND THERE'S BAD NEWS:
The good news is that things are not as they appear.
The real war on terror in Texas is not about "who controls the mid-east oil reserves." The war is against drugs, and the war in not lost in Texas. Fortunately, there is a 100% guaranteed substance abuse preventative, drug addiction relapse in Texas, by *"severing the drug supply at the source".*

A wise man once said that the power of the pen is stronger than mighty armies and all things are possible to those who believe. So the question arises: Does anybody have the courage (FAITH) to publish this consensus throughout the western hemisphere this year? The Apostle Paul wrote

41

what God said in Acts13:23 "I have found David; he will do everything I want him to do."

THROUGHOUT THE SCTIPTURES: The Holy Bible contains many wealthy accounts of God's spectacular men like Noah, Abraham, Joseph, Moses, Joshua, Samson, Gideon, Jonah, Elijah, Daniel, and David also by whom came the linage of our Lord and Savior Jesus Christ. These are all examples by which we can strengthen our faith and also pattern our life's decisions. Through out the scriptures we observe how the enemies of God's children became confused during battle, turning against each other, and completely annihilating them selves.

The Bible describes how the Medianites self-destructed when Gideon intimidated them with a rumor, and then terrified them with distress tactics. With only 300 men, he defeated an army of 135,000 and then slaughtered all their princes as he pursued after the enemy, seizing all the spoils of war. The scripture says: The Spirit of the Lord came upon Gideon and he blew a trumpet. And he sent messengers; and they came up to meet them. Then the Lord said to Gideon, the people that are with thee are too many for me to give the Midianites into their hand, lest Israel vaunt them against me saying mine own hand hath saved me. KJV Judges ch-6 vs-16 "And the LORD said unto him, Surely I will be with thee, and thou shalt *smite the Midianites as one man*."

But now let's consider the great mercies of God after Jonah preached the word of the Lord and warned the wicked city of Nineveh to repent. At first Jonah refused to go preach in Nineveh, but after he was inside the belly of the whale for three days and nights he was glad to go. Then the people believed God and proclaimed a fast, from the greater of them to the least; for the word of the Lord came to the king and he arose from his throne and rent his robe and covered him with sackcloth, and sat in ashes.

And he caused it to be proclaimed; let every man and beast cry mightily to God, yea, let them turn everyone from his evil way. Who can tell if God will turn away His fierce wrath that we perish not. And God saw their works……..

THE BAD NEWS: There are *"millions of drug addict"* throughout America now and so obviously *"just say no"* is not a solution to substance abuse or relapse prevention. Subsequently, there are thousands of offenders imprisoned in (SAFPF) "Substance Abuse Felony Punishment Facilities" throughout the Texas prison system who have a genuine desire for true recovery and yearn after a drug free lifestyle; but if nothing changes, nothing changes. The cruel fact is that a 95% majority of these addicts will relapse again within a very short time of their release from SAFPF units. As long as there is cocaine and heroin available on the street markets in Texas, there will be progressive relapse addictions, resulting in escalated crime rates and untimely deaths.

If you throw a frog into scalding hot water, it will jump out and run off. But if you gently place it into warm water, and slowly turn up the heat, it will boil to death. Such is the paradigmatic complacencies of progressive drug dependency. Consequently on behalf of Texas national security and defense, the main objective is to *"sever the source"* of all illicit drug production that flows thru Texas; breaking the chains of addiction within our Texas national borders, further transforming the tragedy into triumph.

FIERCE FORCE OF UNBRIDLED RETRIBUTION: The drug cartel has firmly established their black-market in the USA, and are now boasting about their $23 billion in annual revenues. Unfortunately, the greed of filthy lucre has stonewalled all referendums. Experts say that the USA politicians will never allow eradication of illicit narcotics trafficking in America because there is too much under-handed money in it for them. Proverbs 17:23 "A wicked man accepts a bribe behind the back to pervert the ways of justice." We stick our heads in the sand in denial as the drug epidemic escalates to unprecedented proportions in America. The USA is sick unto death, as the drug addicts' cravings are stronger than their will to survive, and as this lost generation of substance abusers slip further into chemical dependency.

In a recent scientific experiment with monkeys using cocaine; a perfectly healthy monkey was locked inside a cage and had access to three push-button dispensers. The first-push button was for food, one was for water and one for cocaine. Once the monkey tasted the cocaine, it neglected to take food or water, and just hiatus back to consume more cocaine. Within a few weeks the perfectly healthy monkey died. Subsequently, the Cartel owes Texas, far more restitution than they could ever repay, for exploiting a chronically chemical-dependency, upon our society. But go figure; their accumulated resources should be ample revenue to reimburse our investors and all surpluses will become part of our Texas national heritage to back a new Texas national currency. The policy must always be *"pay the mercenaries as we go"* (no credit-no debt). Money talks, and so therefore, cold hard cash is needed to get the ball up and bouncing. For that reason, sponsorships and investors are imperative to provide the capital venture, because if we don't have the resources available on hand to compensate our *"hired guns"* then we cannot expect to maintain total access to all spoils of war.

—

As Texas has become, the Cartel's main narcotics trafficking corridor now to the USA, by the same token, let's consider this very publication, to be an acronym *"warning of Jonah"*. As the drug lords have continually repudiated the withdraw their contraband from within our borders, a *"fierce force of unbridled retribution"* will soon emerge. There are currently over 154,000 offenders now incarcerated in the Texas Department of Criminal Justice (TDCJ) at any given time; and that's not even counting all the folks on community supervision or those also still detained in county jail facilities, awaiting the rotating door. Should they be afforded one last opportunity to pay retribution?

! EMPLOYMENT OPPORTUNITIES !

Master Strategist is now hiring mercenaries to eradicate narcotics trafficking throughout Texas' jurisdictions. Ex-offenders O.K. Convene online for intelligentsia. Deployment to South America.
PURPOSE: **Redirect the entire Cartel alliance.**
PENALTY: **Destroy all illicit drug production.**
PROFITS: **Seize all the gold, silver, and gems.**
Top pay in pecuniary substance.
Salary plus commission or piece work.
Double pay for Columbia // Peru defection.
Investors and sponsorships needed also.
Respond to: FortunateSoldier@gmail.com

A new military superpower: We all know there is no true victory except that which is won by national arms because otherwise the glory is not authentic and then the wealth falls under further jurisdiction of foreign forces. But TDCJ has access to ample resources and also has the capacity, to instantly recruit, train, and support a new military super-power. Texas national military combat forces must therefore be drafted from within the

—

Texas prison system simultaneously while our own *"soldiers of fortune"* are in route. Eighty five percent (85%) of crime statistics are attributed to drug addictions; obviously, *"dope-fiends"* will do anything for drugs. As usual, all the pessimistic critics ask where the venture capital will come from, but if we stay focused there is always plenty of support for a worthy cause. The investors must always be reimbursed first (do the math) with the Cartel's own wealth and resources. Moreover, if the convict-offenders can man-up and return home clean, sober, and alive, to Texas, they should officially be granted a pardon. Although TDCJ may initially balk at providing resources for the cause, as the phenomenon develops and they consider the benefits, they will all jump on the ban wagon; and if not, that's good enough too, because the Lord's arm is never shortened.

CHOICES, TOLLERANCE & ACCEPTANCE: The USA Today Newspaper reports that: Anybody caught with drugs in Singapore is arrested and severely punished. If caught with certain drugs, the penalty is death by hanging. When you fly into Singapore, it is written on the entry card, "Death to drug traffickers under Singapore law." It is further reported that "street drugs" are virtually unheard of in Singapore. Can you imagine that? They don't have major issues with chemical dependency because it is intolerable and not condoned in their culture. Furthermore, when San JDJesuitas has explored Cuba, he discovered there are no narcotics available on the streets there either. Before his arrival as a tourist, the flight attendants were required, by law, to distribute mandates in writing and further obtain signature acknowledgments from every passenger, regarding the laws and penalties for possession of contraband. The contraband therein described included narcotics and also pornography; both

———

46

of which simultaneously destroy the moral fiber of society. We all know that Castro has been a tyrant and has made immense profits in organized crime. But the laws that still govern in Communist Cuba, do not allow their own people to indulge in such destructive behaviors, because of the subsequent societal devastation.

The USA government turns the blind eye of corruption towards narcotics trafficking throughout this region for decades, but George Bush spends $-trillions-$ to occupy Baghdad. So the US dollar continues to freefall, due to the additional $-trillions-$ deficit with millions of Americans losing their homes to foreign-owned sub-prime lending foreclosures, thus causing the stock market to implode. Democracy is successful only until the voting majority becomes too complacent to govern themselves. Whatever they may choose to condone in NY, LA, or DC does not constitute any prerequisites here in Texas. Freedom for all opposing forces to relocate outside these TEXAS boundaries, is still the freedom of choices, tolerance, & acceptance in Middle-America.

CHATTERING RUMORS: The gold mines are located in Peru; and Columbia also has diamonds, emeralds & rubies. However, the self-serving government administration that controls the resources of illicit drug producing nations, are manipulated by advents of the under-world. Top-dog officials are customarily bought off with bribes, leaving national patriotism void. Hence, the allurement of double-pay will entice the sedition of their private security-forces. These reformation goals can then suddenly be achieved, in sequence, as greed, suspicion and paranoia further wanes the ranks. Thru proper timing, preparation and awareness, Texas national military forces will waylay and ambush the malevolence alliances, and swoop-up the fortune.

THE END

—

Published in Valley Morning Star on August 10, 2011
Vice-Chairman San Glenn

OBITUARY -- Glenn Paul Saufferer of Harlingen, TX went out to meet his creator on Saturday, August 6, 2011. He was born May 20, 1956, to Floyd and Ruth Saufferer, in Harlingen where he lived all his life.

49

He graduated from Harlingen High School in 1975. Glenn lost his wonderful mother Ruth in 1980, but was then blessed with a beloved step-mother, Frances, who had been his great-aunt by marriage so the family had known each other since he was born. He was married for nearly 25 years to Corrina, his first love, who helped him in his carpentry work and also helped him give respite care to his dad, in Floyd's final days.

He is preceded in death by his parents, Floyd and Ruth Saufferer, step-mother, Frances Saufferer, and aunt Charlene Sutherland. He is survived by his brother, Rob Saufferer & wife Jill, nephew Bryan Saufferer & wife Sara, all of Austin, his uncle Paul King Sutherland of Jackson, TN, his former wife Corrina Saufferer of Harlingen, his cousins, Kathy Sutherland Waycaster and Paul Bryant Sutherland, his stepsisters, Judy Maurer, Barbara Breemen and stepbrother, Jim King and by many friends.

Glenn was an amazing carpenter with a creative gift of building cabinets and other beautiful things. He had a knack for seeing things and making them right, in his house and many others. Glenn had a wonderfully quirky sense of humor. He had many friends and a generous heart, always willing to help a friend. He had a love for the outdoors and a recently discovered enjoyment of dancing. Glenn loved history and was interested especially in military history. Glenn loved God with all his heart and is with Him in heaven for eternity. Glenn's one desire is that all his friends will be there with him as well.

Visitation will be held Thursday, August 11, 2011 from 10am to 9pm and the family will receive friends from 6-9pm. Celebration of his life will be held Friday, August 12, 2011 at the Rudy Garza Chapel of Peace at 1:00pm with Pastor Barry Jackson of Christian Fellowship Church officiating and interment will follow at Mont Meta Memorial Park Cemetery. Flowers only last a short time. To celebrate Glenn's life, please seed into something that lasts! In lieu of flowers donations may be made to Outdoor Christian Ministries, www.OCMTX.org, or your favorite charity. Funeral services are under the direction of Rudy Garza Funeral Home of Harlingen.
Sign the guestbook at: http://legacy.com/valleystar/obituaries.asp.

¡OPORTUNIDADES de EMPLEO!

Estratega magistral ahora emplea a mercenarios para erradicar los narco-traficantes de los jurisdicciones a través de Tejas'. Convoque en línea para intelectualidad. El despliegue a Sudamérica; Ex-Ofensores estan bien.

PROPOSITO: Redireccionar la alianza entera de Cártel.
PENA: Destruya toda la producción ilícita de droga.
Las GANANCIAS: Agarre todo el oro, la plata, y las gemas.

El salario más el trabajo de la comisión o el pedazo.
La paga primera en la sustancia pecuniaria.
Paga duplique para la deserción de Columbia y Perú.
Los inversionistas y los patrocinadores necesitaron también.
Responda a: FortunateSoldier@yahoo.com